First published in the United Kingdom 2018.

Copyright © Gina McKie
Publication by © Pan4 Media

A catalogue record of this book is available from the British Library.

ISBN: 978-1-907463-97-6

BEAT
THE BULLY

IMAGINATION

BULLYING HAS BEEN AROUND FOR DECADES

I have ground-breaking news for you, this kind of behaviour will never disappear. The great news is that once it has been recognised, it can be successfully managed.

We all know that bullying exists and some of us choose to ignore it, suffer in silence or raise the alarm. Many of us have experienced this unacceptable behaviour first-hand, and most of us have witnessed it at some point.

Psychological research states that bullying is a type of aggression in which the behaviour is intended to harm or upset a person. This kind of treatment repeatedly occurs over a period of time. There is always an imbalance of power leaving the victim afraid, often terrified. Nowadays I believe that bullying is more prevalent and often unidentified. Cyberbullying is on the increase and the more we can encourage people to come forward and speak out, the better.

I was chatting with my friend the other day about bullying in schools. My friend is a teacher, and I referred to a child as 'badly behaved'. She was horrified I used this expression and told me it was not politically correct to use this phrase. The correct term? 'Kids that have made the wrong choice'! In my book, still badly behaved! However, I think it's encouraging and satisfying to know that systems are constantly being implemented and refreshed in various schools to deal with this kind of behaviour. By law, state schools (not private) must have a behaviour policy in place. This should be standard in all schools, colleges, workplaces etc. Ask for a copy.

If you simply search 'bullying' online you will not be surprised at the amount of helplines and advice there is right at your fingertips. What surprised me is that it is mostly aimed at kids. Of course, we need to address this at an early stage in life before it spills over into adult life. It takes a great deal of time and understanding working with a child (or adult) and their basic emotional and social skills.

Several years ago I presented a late night radio chat show and covered this topic in great detail. We spoke to various callers who were being bullied and wanted help. We changed the detail of every single caller to protect their identity. I will never forget one caller—the bully!

A lady called, and she started our conversation with, "I was a bully; horrible, unkind, thoughtless, but I changed." This lady was not looking for forgiveness but an understanding as to why bullies bully. This is also very important if we believe that people can, and are willing, to change. She explained in great detail that she was being bullied at home and lived in fear of various family members and their torment, adding (which I thought was chilling) that she had no idea what it meant to be 'safe'.

Her way of protecting herself was to quite simply exert power in whatever way she could over others. We all know 'that kid' at school you wanted to avoid. The nasty kid, the bully. This lady was that nasty, indecorous, violent child. Her transformation occurred because she realised her behaviour was inappropriate and if she wanted to have a good friend in life and feel safe, she equally had to offer this.

We all have a turning point in life, and

sometimes you recognise it yourself, and you make it happen, or something extraordinary happens, and change just develops overnight. There is no science attached to this. Some people just wake up and make a decision and adhere to it. Perhaps this is why I often think we can't get caught up in the detail of life. We are never going to solve the world's problems, but we can try. Living your life along the way and having fun, enjoying the journey, that's what is important. As author Ben Sweetland says, *"Happiness is a journey, not a destination."*

Remember, if people are trying to bring you down it only means that you are above them.

> *"If you change the way you look at things, the things you look at change"*
> — Wayne Dyer

How to beat the bully:

Believe In Yourself

Believe that you are a good person and worthy of better treatment. Never seek approval from the bully. Respect yourself and never do something if it makes you feel uncomfortable.

Energy Creates Energy

This might be a challenge (for a time) but you must stay strong and keep your own energy positive and welcoming. People are always attracted to good people. You will attract other (good) people into your life that will support you.

Answer The Bully

Don't be afraid to tell the bully what you are thinking. This is all about control. You are in control of how you respond to their behaviour. If you are unhappy with something they have said or done, tell them.

Talk To Someone You Trust

Silence is not an option. Please talk to someone you trust. There are incredible helplines and services available if you really feel you can't talk to a friend or family member. I would urge you to talk to someone you know and trust.

Track Everything

Record everything. Bullying doesn't just happen overnight. Get yourself a notebook and get writing. Most of us make notes on our phones, tablets, etc but there is something about having 'that little notebook' with your handwritten notes—*magical*. Even today, police officers still record everything in their little notebooks. The power of your handwriting.

Holiday

I am not suggesting you head off to the Bahamas. Give yourself a mental break from this bullying. If you can avoid the bully for a period of time until you can truly reflect on this behaviour, then just do it!

Ending The Relationship

Reassure yourself that this relationship will come to an end. It will. Focus on the other aspects of your life that make you happy. Don't give the bully too much headspace because they are not worth it. It doesn't matter if this person is your friend, partner, colleague, boss...it will end!

Bravery And Your Behaviour

Bullies are clever. It's their game, and they have written the rules. People often say that bullies prey on a particular type. In my experience, I disagree. I have witnessed strong characters being subjected to bullying behaviour. Act with bravery and strength will come your way.

Understand The Situation

Don't dwell on why the bully is 'a bully' but there will be a reason why this person acts in the way they choose to act. If you want to forgive this person, sometimes understanding their background helps.

Laughter In Your Life

The best medicine is laughter. Stay away from the mood hoovers if you need a boost. Watch a great film, go to a comedy show, talk to your 'fun pal'. Never let things get so bad that you are truly unhappy.

Lessons In Life

We all have lessons to learn in life. This period of your life might just be a bad puzzle which you feel you can't solve. What have you learned from this situation which will help you (and maybe someone else) move on? When you solve that puzzle—elation!

You

You are the most important person in all of this. Rule number one, look after number one. It may sound selfish, but you must focus on yourself before you can sort out everything else in your life. It always makes me smile (nervously) when I am on a plane, and the air hostess/steward asks you to put your oxygen mask on 'first' before helping others. It's a simple piece of advice, but simple always works for me. Look after yourself.

> *"Sometimes you will never know the value of a moment, until it becomes a memory"*
> *— Dr. Seuss*

CHANGE
YOUR LIFE
OVER
LUNCH

IMAGINATION

I CHANGED
MY LIFE
OVER LUNCH

And if I had not made a certain decision, I wouldn't be writing this article right now.

I was sixteen years old when I was diagnosed with lupus; an autoimmune disease in which the body's immune system attacks healthy tissue in various parts of the body. I was young, innocent, often bedridden but I was also tenacious and extremely curious. Curiosity has served me well in life, but you have to know when to switch off that 'curious control' or it will control you and spiral quite literally out of control!

For as long as I am on this earth, I will

never forget sitting before a young doctor as she explained to me how I would live my life as a lupus sufferer. There was something about that phrase (lupus sufferer) that instantly made me reject those words and this diagnosis. Medication for life? I didn't believe that I had this debilitating condition. Me? Not possible. Okay, I was taking medication for teenage acne (Minocin), but surely that was not contributing to my ailments? Something just did not feel right. However, doubt is a wonderful seed.

I was prescribed an anti-malaria drug called Hydroxychloroquine and because I was fairly immobile with the pain, steroid injections too. Something inside me challenged all of this. I didn't want to be on medication for life, and the side effects of these drugs started to show quite quickly; hair loss, weight gain, etc.

My brother was the first person to believe

in me. At the time he was studying health and nutrition and worked part-time in a health store. The manager of this health store was a wise woman; there was nothing she didn't know about food and nutrition. I often referred to her as 'Lady Lovely Laura'. She was a lady full of genuine spirit and kindness. Kendon, my brother, introduced us and we met for lunch. A very healthy lunch; dairy-free salad and a glass of aloe vera juice. Instantly I knew I would never stick to this diet. However, I was interested in listening to Laura's views on lupus and whether changing my diet could offer a cure.

As I explained my condition, Laura wrote the list of the pills I was popping. Suddenly she asked me what I thought might happen if I stopped taking all of the drugs. I had no idea, but I was willing to give it a try if it meant no more drug-taking or steroids and finding a healthy replacement (just not bottles of aloe vera juice). Guess what? All of my symptoms disappeared. Completely.

This is the short version of a very complicated story. The seed of doubt over taking Minocin transpired to be the answer. It was Minocin-induced lupus. I had all the symptoms, but the moment I stopped taking this drug, they were gone. To be clear, I queried this on a few occasions with my doctor, but my concerns were dismissed. However, I never dismissed my doubt.

As fate would have it, I stumbled across an article in Laura's health store one day about a young man's acne-drug lawsuit against the manufacturer of Minocin. I contacted his lawyer, and this could have been the start of a very lengthy lawsuit but the thought of filling out a million and one forms to get legal aid and court proceedings frightened the steroids out of me. I was still recovering from lupus, and I decided to use my strength on getting well. I secured a place at Dundee College to study media and radio; this excited me greatly. The road to recovery was in plain sight (in my mind anyway).

That day I had lunch with Laura is a memorable one because I decided I was going to change. Something was going to change, and I knew it would be for the better. It was a huge risk, but I was ready to face whatever was going to happen. I changed my mindset over lunch and took action—the two key ingredients.

There is a reason why so many business deals are made over lunch; bonding with someone, eating nice food and feeling relaxed. Thousands of books have been written covering 'the great deals that are made over great meals'. From *The Art Of The Business Lunch: Building Relationships between 12 and 2'* by Robin Jay to *'Surviving The Business Lunch: 25 Tips in 25 Minutes'* by Carolyn Starry. Intention and purpose are of paramount importance when it comes to having that lunch.

There are five simple steps you should always be aware of if you are thinking of making a great decision over lunch from laughter to leaving on a happy note:

(1): Laughter

Any kind of a lunch where you feel there must be a positive outcome can be awkward and emotionally challenging. Keep it light (I don't just mean the lunch) and friendly. Inject a little humour if possible. Prepare something of interest perhaps that you would like to share.

(2): Understand

Know exactly what you want out of this lunch. You would not sit a test ill-prepared. Prep yourself beforehand with questions, ideas, and most importantly your own guidelines for the outcome you want to achieve.

Sorry. The booze breath can wait. Alcohol impairs our judgement and decision-making. Plus, I have been in many situations where someone has been drinking and promised me the world. Yes, it was the vineyard talking...never happened! If you are in the driving seat of changing your life over lunch, don't drink.

(4): Conversation

If you are having a good conversation, it will flow naturally. Sadly, few people nowadays have time for chit-chat. Keep the chit-chat for after the lunch. The focus is on business (your business) and change. If you asked for the lunch meeting, you pay!

Always end on a happy note. I have a lovely friend who always ends his conversation with, "I will tell you a quick story that will make you feel good before you go." There are two clever parts to this. He is telling me he is ending the conversation, but he is going to make me feel good. I always leave him feeling really good. Keep it positive.

According to the *Institute For The Psychology Of Eating*, you can lose weight too over lunch. Seriously! If you have ever worked hard at trying to shed a few pounds, it takes a lot of work, but that means stress on the body and our metabolism changes very quickly as a result. It has been reported that when people are relaxed (on holiday for example and snacking on all sorts of sweet treats) they actually lose more weight because they are relaxed. This is because we move from chronic sympathetic dominance to a parasympathetic state; our frame of mind has been altered to such an extent that we are able to eat more yet shed a few pounds.

The burning question is, can you really change your life over lunch? Yes, you can. I am not talking about the fun lunch you might have with your friends where you discuss everything from botox to binge-watching your favourite television show. It's a lunch where you know exactly what you want to achieve at the end of it.

George Bernard Shaw once said:

"Change is the law of life. And those who look only to the past or present will miss the future. Progress is impossible without change, and those who cannot change their minds cannot change anything. To improve is to change, to be perfect is to change often."

Often we can't tell the person we love

or care about the most the change we want to make. That is important too. You should explore the conversation on some level with that person.

We have all had lunch on our own at some point. That is a good thing. Time on our own to reflect or perhaps plan. Equally, being around others who want to 'change' is infectious. If you want to be part of a 'change your life over lunch' culture, then register your details via ginamckie.com and I will get back to you. Remember, changing can be a challenge but not changing is catastrophic. Embrace your change.

> *"If you do what you've always done, you'll get what you've always gotten"*
> — Tony Robbins

> *"A person who never made a mistake never tried anything new"*
> — *Albert Einstein*

CONFIDENCE

IMAGINATION

GROWING YOUR CONFIDENCE IS FAIRLY EASY

Many of us spend thousands of pounds attending seminars and coaching sessions, walking on hot coals or broken glass, but it's not that complicated. Just for the record, I have experienced the aforementioned and it was an experience. Just an experience.

I have worked in radio for over twenty years, and it takes confidence to speak on the airwaves every single day. I believe that at some point, everyone should host their own radio show. You learn to listen to your own voice; you might even get to like it! You are showcasing yourself on a daily basis, and you realise that people will judge you on everything you say and the music you play.

I have always been interested in self-development and the power of communication. I have studied psychology, hypnosis and counselling. This has given me a greater understanding of myself and others. I love learning and I am currently studying Cognitive Behavioural Therapy.

Confidence is the best gift you can give yourself. I work with many clients, helping them find and grow their confidence. Here are my top ten tips:

(1): Confidence

Most of the time we are unaware of our confidence until we really need it. If you nurture your confidence on a daily basis, like you would protect yourself in the sun using an SPF, you will invest in your overall happiness and wellbeing. You are responsible for your own confidence. Too many people play the blame game; blaming someone for 'knocking' their confidence. Take control of your internal dialogue and start building your confidence by believing in yourself.

(2): Oral

Talk to yourself in a kind manner. Communication is our ultimate tool in life, and the most important person you should communicate with is yourself. Our lives are so busy nowadays we rarely take time out to ask ourselves what we really want, on a daily basis, monthly basis, etc. We are so easily influenced by the outside world, we don't spend enough time on our own. Quiet time. Reflective time. Time to talk to yourself and guide yourself to your goals in life.

(3): No

Don't be a yes person. No means 'no'.
If you don't want to do something then
don't make excuses, just say no and don't
feel guilty. Powerful people say 'no'
when they need to and don't dwell on
those two tiny letters!

(4): Feelings

Get in touch with your feelings. If you
are feeling uncomfortable, ask yourself
why? You always have the answers
inside you. When you are feeling happy,
acknowledge these moments and remind
yourself of these moments and feelings.
This is a very effective way of maintaining
your happiness too.

(5): Instinct

Thousands of books have been written
on the power of your gut instinct. Do you
really use it? Your gut instinct is your

very own 'sat nav'. The more you use it, this becomes a better guide for you. It's an amazing feeling when something feels right/wrong, and you know how to react.

(6): Delegate

Ask people to do things for you! Some people love serving others and embrace the subservient role. Give praise where praise is due, and in return, you will feel satisfied. If you have confidence in others, they will have confidence in you.

(7): Enrol

Try new things. Push your physical and mental ability. Brian Tracy wrote a wonderful little book called *'Eat That Frog'*. Do the difficult things first in life, and everything else will seem a lot easier.

(8): Nap

When you need to have some shut-eye time, take it. Sometimes we need to rest that racing brain and take some time out to relax. Even just taking five minutes out to listen to your favourite song and closing your eyes can give you an incredible boost.

(9): Care

Do you spend too much time worrying about what people think of you? Start caring for yourself and stop worrying about others. It's a waste of your valuable energy. By following these simple steps, you are caring for yourself!

(10): Energy

Energy goes where the focus flows. Good people have good energy. When your intentions are good, you are giving out good energy but make sure you have some for yourself too. Confidence is an energy. You have probably 'felt' someone's confidence. It's impressive and influential. You have this energy too. Believe it, feel it, and others will see it.

> "Move out of your comfort zone. You can only grow if you are willing to feel awkward and uncomfortable when you try something new"
> — Brian Tracy

> "Everything you want is on the other side of fear"
> — Jack Canfield

ENJOY
THE
WINTER
MONTHS

IMAGINATION

ENJOY THE WINTER MONTHS AND PREPARE FOR A NEW YOU

Accept the fact or should I say 'fat' that you are going to put on a few extra pounds over the winter months. The moment I feel that 'extra roll' on my body I promise myself, every year, that the diet will start tomorrow, but one more chocolate from the Roses tin won't do much harm.

This is normally the start of my stress cycle; diet, cleaning the house, bills, work and the list goes on and on. I recognise this stress sequence and never allow it to spiral out of control. Over-thinking is easy, taking control of it can be a challenge, but you can do it.

I am quite sure sales of Paul McKenna's book *'I Can Make You Thin'* soar at this time of year. I disagree with that title. The emphasis should certainly not be on 'thin'. If you are naturally thin, lucky you. My friend could eat double chocolate cheesecake swimming in double cream all day long and not gain one pound. I just need to get a whiff of it before I feel my bingo wings expanding. I prefer the title, *I Can Make You ThinK!*

Thinking is easy but to get results you must take action. Positive praying and positive affirmations are wonderful but they operate at the surface level of your conscious thinking. You have to dig much deeper and in order to do so, you need a plan.

Decisive self-talk is great if you are making plans. Knowing what you want and taking control of your intentions. The problem with most of us is that our self-talk is negative and self-deprecating. We never get beyond the 'I can't really do this' attitude. Before we know it, we have talked ourselves out of achieving what we started thinking about in the first place.

Our lives are based on seeking happiness and avoiding pain. In her exercise videos, Jane Fonda made the phrase 'no pain, no gain' famous. Most of us like the comfort zone and to get out of that space you have to push yourself that little further. This often requires a bit of discomfort along the way.

Recently I was in Vienna, and I visited the home of Sigmund Freud. What a wonderful experience. A beautiful old-fashioned flat full of books and memories. I read a little bit about Freud's theory on how we approach life. His belief was that there are two guiding methods by which we can approach life. The pleasure-pain principle or the reality principle.

Avoiding pain and seeking pleasure is one way—we simply bypass the stuff we don't like and select the good things. The reality principle is where you would deliberately embrace a painful experience in order to get the gains later. Delayed gratification.

There is a wonderful little book called *Eat That Frog* by Brian Tracy, as I explained earlier. Brian pretty much tells you to do the things you don't want to do (but you know you need to) FIRST! After that, everything is a little simpler. I apply this philosophy and logic when I am tackling my ironing every Sunday night. I always do the shirts first!

Right now I am sure you can think of something you need to do, but it's on that dusty old shelf in the back of your mind. Bring it to the forefront of your mind for a few seconds. Indeed, say it out loud. Make it real. Make a plan. Make it happen. When are you going to do something about this?

You can read this article and do nothing. Or, you can read this and actually grasp the things you need to do. By tackling the things you really need to do you simply make room for great opportunities.

People often talk about turning their life around. It starts with a decision then action. Don't let another year pass and you are still saying the same thing, or you feel as if you haven't achieved anything.

Even if you start by tidying out that bottom drawer! Perhaps you will find that key you have been searching for, or maybe you will come across a phone number for an old friend. Imagine the conversation you might have and where that might take you? Don't live in your head, get ahead by taking action.

Make That Call

There is always someone we need to call. It might be a friend or the bank but make that call. Get it off your list. Also, this is a lonely time of year for many people. Your call could change their day!

Tidy That Wardrobe

You might think it's tidy but when did you last do a proper assessment of what you really need and wear? If you haven't worn something for a long period of time, get rid of it! Give it to your local charity shop.

Your Finances

We can all save money if we just take the time to really look at our finances. Be your own financial expert and if you are not making any extra money, find ways of saving money.

I love **moneysavingexpert.com**

Healthy Eating Plan

It really does make a difference when you consciously keep track of what you are eating. That extra latte and muffin you had? It all adds up. Write it down. Keep a diary. Note what you would like to change and make that change.

Christmas Decorations

Don't put decorations away that you know are tired or you don't really like. Make this the year you are ruthless with what you are storing away until next year.

Walk and Talk

The best therapy! Make time to get out of the house with your friend or partner. Your good friends are your best counsellors. We all have worries but sharing them and dealing with them is the only way to avoid stress. It might feel stressful at the time but remember, no pain, no gain.

Learn Something New

Learn a new word or do a daily quiz, just expand that wonderful mind you have. The only way your mind will develop is if you challenge it.

The Power of Giving

Do something nice for someone and don't tell anyone. It's a powerful thing to do and the universe will look after you. Do it for no other reason than simply sharing your kindness.

Comedy

Make sure you have fun in your life. Watch a funny film or search for some great comedy clips online. Something to make you smile.

Be Proud

Be proud of yourself. Too often we don't appreciate ourselves and the little things we might do for others that might just make their day. It's the little things that always count. Take a moment every now and then where you can reflect on what you have achieved. Be proud of the past and excited about your future.

> "Nothing is impossible. The word itself says *'I'm possible!'*"
> — Audrey Hepburn

FACE
YOUR
FEAR

IMAGINATION

There is a huge difference between a fear and a phobia

We all have intrinsic fears, and then there are crippling phobias that really do prevent some people from living a normal (whatever that is nowadays) standard of life.

I have always been interested in helping people overcome their fears/phobias but above all, helping them find their inner-confidence in order to push their own boundaries. You can do it too! Sometimes we have set boundaries for ourselves, and we don't even know they exist. It's only when we are confronted with a particular challenge that we experience the fight or flight mode. It's not that complicated to

47

face your fear and turn your life around. We often make it more complicated in our own heads. I believe that fear means **'Fantasied Evidence Appearing Real'**. In the same way we use our imaginations to create a fear, we can use our powerful imaginations to unravel that fear.

From the moment we are born, we only fear two things. The fear of falling and the fear of loud noise. If you are familiar with neuro linguistic programming, then you will know the importance of programming your own brain in order to achieve what you really want in life. Most people just don't believe in their own potential.

What the mind can conceive, the body will achieve. I can say this with great confidence because I have worked privately with hundreds of clients, helping them face their fears. Whether it's a fear of public speaking or a fear of flying, the underlying issues are often very similar and normally involve the threat of a panic attack.

I worked with a lady a few years ago, and she had a fear of crossing the Kingston Bridge in Glasgow. She was involved in a bad accident several years ago and couldn't face returning to the location of the accident. The short version of this story is that I shared with her some of the tools and techniques (I will share with you too) that I have developed over the years. As a hypnotherapist, I deepened some of these techniques in her subconscious mind. The following day she called me to tell me that she didn't cross the Kingston Bridge once, she crossed it ten times! She amazed herself. I wasn't surprised at all. Dare I say, we all have bridges to cross and sometimes we just need a little bit of encouragement, perhaps a little more depending on the size of the bridge.

Meet Des. Des should be your best friend. **Diet, Exercise,** and **Sleep**. Every single day you should be aware of **Des.** This is the basic formula to give you traction in life. Really keep you on the right tracks. Then, there is the magic within you. Here are some tools to help you face your fear, find your inner-magic and boost your confidence.

Movement

If you are facing a fear, get moving. Move that body. Even if it's just walking. You can only burn so much energy and when you are nervous about something, sitting and worrying about it is worse. I don't use a chaise longue when I am working with a client. Yes, I have one, but I often walk with my clients. If you can get outside and experience fresh air, even better. Get moving!

Ask

Ask yourself (yes, it's okay to talk to yourself) what you are afraid of. Write it down. What advice would you give to a friend? Your own advice is often the best answer. There is a reason why people say 'the answer' is always within you. Don't Google the answer, think for yourself. This is about connecting with yourself and understanding what makes you tick.

Gear

Get in gear. What changes do you need to make to change direction, overcome your fear? If you could make one small change right now, what would it be? Change your thoughts, change your direction. If you always do what you have always done, you will always get what you have always got. Make sense?

Inner-dialogue

I talk about this a lot with my clients. Don't allow that pesky little voice in your head to take over. You know the voice, the one that can cause your heartbeat to race uncontrollably. Quite literally, tell it to shut up! A relaxed mind will create relaxed reactions. Remind yourself of a lovely experience, kind words someone said to you, a favourite scene from a film. Just try and relax that mind, this will get good thoughts flowing.

Create

You are the creator of you. So, create good thoughts and a positive outlook. You don't need to have a vision board displayed in your bedroom! Plenty of my clients show me their boards, but if they don't hold the vision of what they want clearly in their own minds, they will never gravitate towards their goals. Store your amazing vision board in your mind. Make it so clear, that when you close your eyes, it lights up your mind and you can see (maybe experience) every detail. This is also very powerful when you are feeling anxious. Get drawing in your mind on that vision board, creating the perfect outcome for you.

> *"Don't wait. The time will never be just right"*
> — Napoleon Hill

THE
ART OF
MANIPULATION

IMAGINATION

Have you ever done something for someone and instantly regretted doing it?

Of course you have! Did you ever consider that you were 'being manipulated'? It's a clever technique and one which many will view as being selfish, inconsiderate and perverse.

Knowing how to do this and recognising it in others is paramount if you want to be a meritorious manipulator—someone who is actually admired for always getting what they want.

Magicians are master manipulators. Many years ago I interviewed the late Paul Daniels. We spoke about manipulation and he sold the idea to me as a fun, acceptable, skill in the world of magic. Yet many people dislike magicians as they view their skill as downright trickery. Trickery, perhaps, but the magician always gets the outcome he desires.

There are 'menipulators' and 'womenipulators'. Those who use their sexuality to get what they want. Whether it is wit, charm, looks or locks, they will use their charisma to charm you and manipulate you. If you select this technique, you will alienate many people around you. It's impossible to flirt with everyone, and most people know that flirtation equals attention with intention.

Manipulating someone without their realisation is the skill. This is where it's time to get emotional. If you are appealing to someone's I.Q. (rather than their E.Q.) you won't succeed at every turn. You must tap into their sensitive side, win them over, and then strike.

There are various techniques from 'playing the victim' to the 'bribery technique'. Playing the victim can leave you in a vulnerable position in the long term. This is where you may use some kind of pitiful excuse to make someone feel sorry for you; then you take action.

The bribery technique is a popular method of manipulating someone. Beware of Greeks bearing gifts, as they say. If you understand how this works, you can use it to your advantage. We don't want to believe however that every single time we are given a gift, there is also an ulterior motive. If you are nonetheless working your M.S. (manipulation skills) you will give a gift, normally a random gift out of the blue, and then return a few days later with your request.

A common sales technique is using time, or lack of it, to your advantage. A hard sell—you have probably heard that phrase. In many instances, it works because the manipulator puts the pressure on their target and forces them to believe that action must be taken NOW. This is effective if there is trust and respect between both parties.

Manipulators are often regarded as 'psychological bullies'. Nobody wants that title but most people want to believe that there is a little bit of magic within them. An unknown energy that creates a sprinkling of fairy dust, creating exactly what you want before your very eyes. Abracadabra…which quite literally translates as 'I create as I speak'. In other words, pick your words carefully.

Overall, the key ingredients are what you say, how you say it and when you say it. A good communicator is always respected. Believing in your outcome is half the battle. If there is any doubt in your self-belief, you will create distance. A bond must be created between you and your (let's say) candidate before you can work your skills. Build bonds, be strong, practice persuasiveness and work your inner-magic.

> *"Life is like riding a bicycle. To keep your balance, you must keep moving"*
> — Albert Einstein

OVERCOMING
GRIEF

IMAGINATION

Overcoming grief
of any kind
is a challenge

Grief is a natural response to loss. We are programmed to deal with it, but until it happens to you, you have probably never operated that programme.

If there is one phrase you don't want to hear when you are in the midst of grieving, it is that 'time is a great healer.' Yes, it is, but when this is mentioned to someone who is trying to overcome grief, it feels as if that time is infinite. There is no magic formula for overcoming grief; it's managing your grief that will help you reach that final stage of 'acceptance' — another word you don't want to hear in the early stages of mourning your loss.

One friend who had lost her elder sibling some months before was asked on a night out. When she said she wasn't ready, the friend who had invited her said, "Life goes on." My friend's point was that for her sibling it doesn't. Grief is not linear in terms of time but jagged and can continue to scar.

Whether you are religious or not, you must believe and accept that your loved one is at peace; resting in peace. We say it but believing it truly is key to moving on. Rest In Peace: it's a global belief of hope and acceptance in our own minds.

Many therapists and books will tell you about the different stages of grief, and this can be overwhelming if you have just lost a loved one. The first stage is simple, let it all out! Anger, hurt, pain—face your feelings, *don't put a face on.*

In 1969, psychiatrist Elisabeth Kübler-Ross introduced what became known as the *'Five Stages of Grief.'* These stages of grief were based on her studies of the feelings of patients facing terminal illness, but many people have generalised them to other types of negative life changes and losses, such as the death of a loved one or a break-up.

The five stages of grief:

*Denial:
"This can't be happening to me."

*Anger:
"Why is this happening? Who is to blame?"

*Bargaining:
"Make this not happen, and in return I will ____."

*Depression:
"I'm too sad to do anything."

*Acceptance:
"I'm at peace with what happened."

Dealing With Denial

At this stage, you may have many unanswered questions leaving you confused and isolated. Talk to someone you trust: a good listener. There is only so much you can talk about before you start repeating yourself and this is the process/cycle you must stop. Write down your questions. Leave them for a day or so and then try to answer those questions yourself. We always have the answers within us.

Tackling Anger

I have a new technique and it works, or at least it has worked for those I have worked with recently. Listen to yourself in this state. Record yourself. It's easy to install an app on your phone, tablet and so on that will do this, even if it's a case of leaving your anger outburst on your own answering machine. When you are calm, listen to this message and you will be surprised at your reaction. You will give yourself good advice.

Bargaining

There are no deals to be made. It is that simple. You can ask for peace and contentment. The universe works in magical ways. Thoughts are things. Think of positive outcomes and believe that you will stop hurting. You must try to see a positive bright future. We talk about a bright future because that is how you must see this in your mind—lots of colour. Create that picture.

Damn That Depression

Aside from taking medication, there are so many ways to overcome depression. The most important part here is recognising that you might be in this state. The good news is, it won't last. Keep busy and get out in the fresh air. Sleep, diet, and exercise will keep you on the right track.

Acceptance

I don't think the journey ever ends if you have truly loved someone. If you love deeply, you hurt deeply. Over time, you let go of the hurt and desire to still be with your loved one. Memories are no longer painful but a pleasant reminder of what you once had. A broken heart is difficult to mend, but I believe that when we love again, a new heart (spiritual) grows. Like a flower, that keeps flowering. You will love again.

"Grief is not linear in terms of time but jagged and can continue to scar"
— Gina McKie

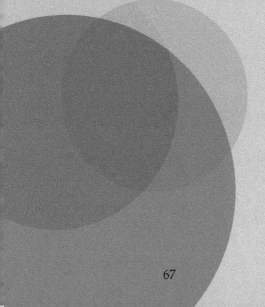

"If you think you are too small to make a difference, try sleeping with a mosquito"
— Dalai Lama

PHD:
PERSONAL
HAPPINESS
DEVELOPMENT

IMAGINATION

Your Very Own PHD 'Personal Happiness Development'

There are some people, and you probably know one or two, who embrace unhappiness. Yes, that's right. They love to wallow in their own self-pity. When you enter into their dark dialogue, you start to feel unhappy too.

The road to misery is an easy one if you allow yourself to digest their moans and groans. We all have them but how we react to them and manage them is life's challenge.

I always laugh when I read the statistic that 'children laugh 300/400 times a day and adults only laugh 17.5 times per day' (don't forget the .5 or statisticians will have a meltdown moment). Let's think about this. If it was true then children awake 12 hours per day would be laughing at least once every 1-2 minutes from sunrise till sunset. For adults, who really knows? What we can deduce from this is that kids, in general, laugh more than adults. Do we have less laughter as we get older? Well, that is up to you. Like anything in life, I believe that you have to work at your happiness. Most of us want the quick fix; the glass of wine, comfort food or some form of psychotropic medication.

As a hypnotherapist and confidence coach, I often work with clients who are just 'unhappy'. Most are surprised and irate when I tell them it's their own fault.

This is never a good start but I like to get into the discomfort zone and stay there for a while. Of course, nobody wants to feel uncomfortable, but that feeling never lasts. An unhappy marriage, a boring job, disagreements with friends/family often top the list of why someone is 'just unhappy'. This is why change is so important. If you don't make changes emotionally and physically you will never be happy with your life.

Guess what, it's your life and you are in charge! Take charge and lose the fear of the unknown. Easier said than done but the small steps lead to the huge leaps, life-changing experiences. How often have you heard a story about someone who has completely turned their life around? Well, why not you?

A client recently said to me that she had experienced a night of misery and couldn't get certain images out of her head. She was desperately unhappy. She explained in great detail how she cried uncontrollably after watching the movie *Sophie's Choice*. If you have never seen this movie, it's a tearjerker starring Meryl Streep who was forced to choose which of her two young children would be sent to the gas chamber when the family was imprisoned in Auschwitz. Well, my client had a choice. To play another movie in her head (a classic comedy) or keep playing the same sad movie in her head again and again. My client explained that she found this difficult, replacing the images with happy ones. Working towards happiness can be a challenge, but you have to work at it. After an hour of 'happy talking' she left with a smile on her face. I think she forgot to be unhappy. The power of distraction is a wonderful tool.

The ultimate goal in life is always happiness. Whatever you might be searching for, the end result is 'if it makes you happy...' (Sheryl Crow even sang about it). This is why I have developed the happiness handbook (available later this year) but I will share some simple steps with you.

Firstly, is there a science in being happy? An actual formula. I believe so. Major advances in neuroscience have revealed some incredible facts about our brains being the true home of our feelings. You might wear your 'heart on your sleeve' but your brain is controlling all emotions. It's romantic to say you love someone with 'all of your heart'. It paints a perfect picture. If you said, 'all of your brain'… it's just not the same.

CBT *(Cognitive Behavioural Therapy)* shows us that we can change the way we think and feel by repeated exposures to thinking positive, healthy, thoughts. Thus, strengthening the left prefrontal cortex (the feel-good part of the brain). Know that you can work on your own brain without spending hours in therapy. Kickstart your own PHD!

'Hi-Five Yourself'!

Say hi to your five simple steps to maintaining a happy brain. **Do this on a regular basis:**

(1): Watch a TED Talk—ted.com

Watch an inspirational talk. There are plenty of short ones. This will get your brain in gear, challenging your thoughts and emotions. These talks are excellent: technology, entertainment, and design.

(2): Exercise

This is a must on a daily basis. We all know that exercise releases endorphins. Get walking even for twenty minutes. You must take time-out.

(3): Happy quotes

There are millions of happy quotes on the internet. Read a few and devise your own. It's our duty to add to the world of happy quotes or we will consistently rely on the classics.

"Happiness is the most important thing in the world, without it you live a life of depression"
—Marilyn Monroe

(4): Say Something Nice and Meaningful

Be genuine and honest with someone. It might even be a stranger. You might just make someone's day.

(5): Face The Mirror

Look in the mirror and like what you see. When we look in the mirror we tend to be looking for faults or that stray hair that requires plucking. Like what you see. Scientists are actually working on a mirror that will soon be able to detect certain illnesses from the fatty tissues in your face. If you are going to look in this mirror, you may as well be happy.

TALKING
TOXIC

IMAGINATION

If you have ever lost your mobile phone or somehow deleted various contacts, you will possibly have faced a slight panic attack

I can still remember the hot flush that raced through my body as I accidentally erased everything from my mobile phone. Momentarily, a surge of relief swept over me as I reassured myself 'everything will be stored in The Cloud'. A 'back-up', that's all I need to do.

I was working through my own mental thunderstorm, feeling as if I had just wiped out my entire world of friends/contacts, desperately trying to find a solution for a full restore to my phone. I should add at this point that I had suddenly split from my partner, and I was living with my brother, his wife, and newborn baby. I didn't want anyone to know where I was living. Suddenly, I had a moment of clarity that changed my life.

My mindset shifted from a stage of chaos to calm. Quite literally in a heartbeat. Always worth remembering you can change your 'state' in a heartbeat. Rather than panicking about trying to contact everyone stored in my phone, I made a decision that I would only ever store someone's details if they contacted me. Yes, I am the kind of person who suddenly thinks of someone I haven't contacted for a long time and will send a text, or call, just to say 'hi'. I love when I get a message like this. No ulterior motive, just a genuine message from someone asking about my wellbeing. Treasure these people!

This loss of contacts changed my life, those in it and my view of people who really care about you. As I was reassessing my entire life (aside from the bitter break-up and finding a place to stay) I discovered I had a toxic friend. You will have one too, and perhaps you have never thought about it but allow me to elucidate.

Nothing feels better than a good clean out of your wardrobe, that bottom drawer, your desktop...whatever it might be, but we very rarely do this with our friends. Should we have some kind of a 'friendship cull'? Absolutely. If you want to spend quality time with people who really care for you, get rid of the toxic ones. Brutal, perhaps, but liberating. This is about your inner-pride and self-esteem, both of which will increase when you let go of those who are surprisingly suppressing your personal success, and you don't even realise it.

There is a belief that you can fit your true friends into a phone box. A true friend you can rely on 24/7. Someone who doesn't judge you, respects your space and will support you when times are tough. The toxic friend may appear to possess these characteristics until you ask for their help. You won't get it. Selfishness will intervene, and excuses will be offered.

A toxic friend might also be a family member. A family member doesn't mean you need to accept their friendship. Some people love to control others and will make you feel guilty if you don't adhere to their rules. They may try to make you feel self-centred if you don't comply with family needs. I call these people *'Toxic Takers'*, always taking from you but never repaying.

Drinkers will always seek out other

drinkers. A toxic friend will encourage you to drink rather than tell you that your drinking is excessive. They are social butterflies and will flirt from one friendship to the next. This is the kind of friend you can't trust. They will use the information you might pour out over a glass of Sauvignon Blanc at another stage.

We all have friends for different reasons, but the toxic friends also stop you from forming new good relationships. You may have been Sally's best pal in primary 4, but that doesn't mean you need to maintain that friendship for old time's sake. This also might be the perfect friendship and that is wonderful. You have to trust and listen to your gut instinct.

When a relationship with a partner comes to an end it can be heartbreaking or the fresh start you need. We let go, eventually in some cases, and move on. An emotionally healthy person will let go. A toxic person (this can be your partner too) won't allow you to progress. The same way you wouldn't tolerate (or shouldn't) any nonsense from a partner, is exactly the same way you manage the toxic friend out of your life. All relationships have an expiry date. Most of us want that friend or partner for life but the reality is that it will end at some point. There is no timescale for the perfect relationship. Some are just shorter than others. Each relationship or friendship is a journey of some sort; just don't let the toxic ones poison you along the way.

Five simple steps to identifying the toxic one:

(1): Identify the Toxic One

First, you need to really think about your friends and your relationship with each individual. If you were running a business, you would select the good ones and weed out the bad ones. Organise your circle of friends like you are running your own friendship business. Some people are not loyal to you, they are loyal to their need of you. When their needs change so does their loyalty.

(2): Tell Them, and Don't Feel Ashamed

Few of us embrace confrontation. This is about believing in yourself and respecting yourself. If you want a good friend, you have to be a good friend. If you believe that you are a good friend, it's time to share this with the person you feel is not a valuable friend. Air and share your views and if you don't feel the relationship improves, start creating your distance.

(3): Focus on Your Good Friends

Good friends won't gossip about other good friends. The toxic friends will gossip about others and treat others disrespectfully. The toxic friends might stop you from spending time with those worthy of your friendship. Make friends with people who force you to level up. Dismiss those who bring you down as they are already below you.

(4): Be Prepared for the Backlash

It's a challenge not to respond to cheeky messages. It might be a text message or email, perhaps a random comment on social media. You must try to ignore any rude provocations. Focus on future friendships, not the past. Of course this can be difficult but you must not waste your time on this. You wouldn't watch a movie that you disliked time and time again, so stop replaying or focussing on any kind of a backlash.

(5): Put Yourself First, and be Proud Doing So

If you firmly believe that you are a good friend, good people will always gravitate towards you so don't worry about losing a few friends along the way if you think they are toxic. Some friends will talk to you in their free time, and others will free their time to talk to you. Start to notice the next time someone calls you, how you feel, your initial response. Sighing is lying; if you sigh before you answer the call but put on a brave friendly face/tone, you are only causing yourself distress. Your time is too precious, so start spending it with those you know really care about you.

"If you want a good friend, you have to be a good friend"
— Gina McKie

THE
POWER
OF
LOVE

IMAGINATION

Love Hurts, Love Kills, Love Will Tears Us Apart, Love Will Keep Us Together, Love Is The Drug

Have I hit a chord with you yet? I adore all of these songs and the power behind the lyrics.

Love is a powerful drug but do we really know just how powerful? Many of us love being in love and others fear this incredible feeling. Is it possible to control love? Can you really die of a broken heart?

A heavy heart, a turbulent tummy, loss of appetite…falling in love takes over our entire bodies but what the heck is actually going on in our brains?

Psychologists have shown it takes between 90 seconds and 4 minutes to decide if you fancy someone. Research has shown this has little to do with what is said. 55% is through our body language, 38% is tonality, and 7% is through what we say.

Doctor Helen Fisher is a biological anthropologist based at Rutgers University in America. She has proposed three stages of love: lust, attraction, and attachment. Each stage being driven by various chemicals in our bodies. Perhaps if we understand the science behind 'love' we can control this mighty emotion.

Lust is a pulling power, drawing you into a world of excitement and desire. This is the first stage of love and is driven by the sex hormones testosterone and oestrogen, in both men and women. This feeling makes you want to touch someone, connect with them, get close and heighten that emotion.

The second stage of falling in love is attraction. This is the incredible time when you are love-struck and can think of little else. You know you are obsessing but somehow can't help yourself. Scientists think that three main neurotransmitters are involved in this stage: adrenaline, dopamine, and serotonin.

Have you ever noticed that when you first meet your new love (those first few dates) your heart races, you stumble over your words and you might even sweat a little? You can thank Mr. Adrenalin for this. This is your stress response and cortisol plays a part too.

Dopamine stimulates desire and reward by triggering a rush of intense pleasure. It has the same effect on the brain as taking certain Class A drugs. Yes, this feeling is addictive and naturally we want to chase this feeling.

Serotonin is one of love's most important chemicals giving us feelings of happiness and well-being. It is involved in mood, appetite, sleep, and emotion. Whenever you are with your new 'love' or you even think of this person, the nice feelings appear. Serotonin could play a role in why we love chocolate so much—chocolate contains tryptophan, which is a chemical that the brain uses to make serotonin.

No wonder some people think that love is complicated—it is! We are emotional creatures, that's what makes us human. We love being in love, but the complications around being in love often come from our own insecurities or feelings of boredom with a new partner. Most of the time, it's not boredom, it's balance. When we really get to know someone, fall for someone, everything appears to be balanced (chemically). This takes us to the next stage, attachment.

Attachment in a relationship is that moment you suddenly feel totally connected to your new squeeze. You don't question the fact you are 'in a relationship' or in love with this person, it's all about acceptance and creating a future. This is often a scary stage for those who have suffered rejection in the past.

Scientists believe that there are two major hormones involved in this feeling of attachment: oxytocin and vasopressin.

Oxytocin is often referred to as the cuddle hormone. It is released by men and women during orgasm creating feelings of closeness and contentment. The more sex a couple has, the deeper their bond becomes.

Vasopressin is the monogamy chemical in our bodies. Only about 3% of mammals are monogamous. Here is the worrying part, humans are not one of these naturally monogamous creatures. The prairie vole is monogamous. It is this little animal responsible for our knowledge of this chemical.

Unrequited love is a horrible feeling. Sam Smith's number one album, *In The Lonely Hour*, is all about this. Idolising your partner can be dangerous. Nobody is perfect and this is where love can be blind. The power of loving yourself should help you move on and let go of someone who doesn't feel the same. This is why it's so important to be yourself in a relationship. Someone else will love you for just being you.

We often hear of a partner passing away shortly after their loved one had died. Bereavement can have a direct effect on the health of the heart. According to the British Heart Foundation, there is a temporary condition where your heart muscle becomes suddenly weakened or stunned. The left ventricle, one of the heart's chambers, changes shape. A broken heart?

My dear friend Belinda says that she has never fallen in love. The idea of falling in general is negative, perhaps suggesting that there is a sense of losing control. She argues that we rise to love, we are elevated in some way giving one another feelings of worthiness. An interesting look at being in love. So, do you rise or fall? If love makes the world go round, we should embrace it and share it. Above all, understand it and its power. It can be mystical and magical but there is a science behind it. Maybe we shouldn't analyse it too much. When we are falling in love, we should just fall and let it all fall into place. In the words of ABC, *Love Conquers All*.

THE
INTERVIEW

IMAGINATION

Many years ago, when I was a young producer

I watched an interview take place in a radio studio and I made myself a promise at the end of this awkward interview; if ever someone didn't really want to talk with me or engage in any kind of conversation, I would politely end the interview. Or, as we would say in the business, 'wind it up'.

The graceless guest will remain anonymous. Not because I don't want a lawsuit on my desk tomorrow morning but because I don't want the focus to be on him — oh, slight clue there! Yes, it was a male star who was popular in the 80s as an actor and a singer/songwriter. He was a rude, arrogant guest and I have never witnessed my colleague be so flustered in my entire career.

An interview, for me, should always feel natural. Indeed, I'm even uncomfortable with the word 'interview'. In my experience, the best conversations happen when you absolutely connect with that person. The term 'an interview' as such reminds me of my college days where we were told to prepare a list of questions, get the answers and report the interview. Perhaps this format didn't help my colleague when he was ready to interview **'Celebrity A'** (*Celebrity Awkward*).

I was rather excited to meet this television star too until I was in the studio watching the frosty interview take place. 'Celebrity A' decided to read a newspaper as my colleague tried to ask him questions.

As he turned each page, my colleague would ask another question until the guest eventually quirked, "Are these the best questions you have?" It was not my job to intervene but in my head I had that Ally McBeal moment of what I would do, my reaction. It was not pleasant and I shocked myself with a few obscenities! Best left in my head. I do remember walking with this 'star' back to his tour bus as I escorted him out of the building. We never exchanged words, though he fully engaged in a conversation with his personal assistant.

I can't remember the specific details of my colleague's response; I merely remember he suddenly became a bumbling wreck before my very eyes. Completely out of character! That was the moment I promised myself I would never allow someone else to reduce me to that sorry state.

I have interviewed many incredible

celebrities over the years from Kylie, Phil Collins to Sir Cliff Richard. Throughout my twenty odd years in media, I have never encountered 'the awkward interview' until recently.

I was scheduled to interview a well-known television presenter who appears on various cooking programmes. I tend to think of him a chef but he is not. He is opinionated, articulate and his own culinary skills are excellent. I interviewed him last year and I did wonder if he might remember me again.

As I started the interview, he appeared to be rather resistant. Constantly looking at his P.R. agent, asking why he had to rush to do a pre-recorded interview? I attempted to talk about his early days in the business. Again, he didn't look at me. He continued to throw questions at his P.R. agent making everyone feel anxious with his impatient behaviour. I stopped the interview.

The promise I made myself years ago gave me the confidence to tell him that I sensed there was clearly a problem and if he didn't want to continue, bye-bye. Simple. I took a deep breath as my producer (boss) remained poker-face watching our conversation unfold.

Whenever I am slightly nervous, I over talk — tangent talking! I started to tell him that as a 'reiki master' I dislike negative energy. Suddenly, I found myself telling him about the 'experience' twenty-odd years ago. Talk about suppressed feelings.

In a heartbeat, the energy changed. He never apologised, he suddenly became the character I watch and like on telly: fun, assertive, but friendly and willing to talk. He delivered an impressive interview, giving me a big hug at the end and reassured me if I ever wanted to chat to him again it was not a problem. For his benefit or mine?

I think we have all experienced that moment when you are talking to someone and you know they are not that interested in YOU! They might even glance over your shoulder, ask you about someone else (trying to get information), you get the drift... I have a simple rule, don't waste your time with these people. Above all, don't let them make you feel as if you need to try harder to impress them in order to fully engage.

It's a wonderful feeling when someone is interested in you, genuinely interested. They make you feel special by asking you about your feelings, your family, work and so on.

Maybe you are that person who has that ability to make someone feel exceptional and important? If someone makes you feel like this, spend your valuable time with them.

I meet so many amazing people

in my job and the most interesting people are those who are consistent, respectful, genuine and trustworthy. The successful celebrities/people ooze these characteristics.

The said interviewees I have mentioned are not bad guys. Still, manners cost nothing. If Oprah had conducted these interviews, the outcome I am sure would be rather different.

I say this time and time again but life is too precious to spend time with people who are just not that interested in you. They will display their affections elsewhere, and you may crave a piece of this attention. If you feel as if you are the one always maintaining the relationship, you are!

Don't fall for the *Red Carpet Characters* in life. Those who know the difference between when it's lights, camera, action and then when the lights are off and the camera ain't rolling. We are all on that red carpet in life. We should all feel special when someone wants to talk to us or shake our hand for whatever reason. You ask questions, they ask questions and the conversation just flows. Nowadays, the cameras are always rolling and true colours always emerge.

"If you feel as if you are the one always maintaining the relationship, you are!"
— Gina McKie

"A lot of people are afraid to say what they want. That's why they don't get what they want"

— Madonna

THE
LAW
OF
ATTRACTION

IMAGINATION

Do you believe that you attract into your life what you really want? I do

Positive or negative, whatever we think about is a magnet to whatever is out there in this great universe.

Yes, you can break it down on a scientific level that we are walking, talking vibrational transmitters operating on a universal frequency. Yet, science can't explain the existence of conscious minds. The simple fact is that thoughts are things. If this is the case, can we really use our minds as magnets to attract what we want? Surely it's worth trying!

I have worked in radio for over twenty years and I sit with my best bud Mike for five hours nearly every single day. (Mic, the microphone) and I imagine quite clearly just one person who might be listening. I may connect with them via the airwaves but perhaps there is some kind of extra-sensory perception going on too. You would be surprised at the amount of times I think of a song I would like to play, and it's suddenly requested by a listener.

My father is a retired police officer and served in the C.I.D. for many years. He had a demanding job and my mum was often left disappointed when dad would call to say he couldn't come home because he had to work. No, he wasn't having an affair! I remember thinking, I will never marry a cop! *Surprise Surprise*, Cilla could have possibly predicted this — I married a cop.

So, is the negative thought stronger than

the positive thought? I don't think anyone truly knows that answer. It's what you are thinking about that will come into your life in some shape or form, that is for sure.

Most importantly, connect with yourself. Listen to yourself and your thoughts. You are always in control. If you don't like what is on the radio, you switch stations or turn it off. Someone else will still be listening though — that frequency is still operating.

You have chosen to disconnect because you are out of sync with what is going on around you.

When peace and harmony are around you (and it's paramount that you recognise this) you possibly don't even think about it.

Learn to recognise when you are in sync (stable equilibrium) because this is your happy state too. When you are content, you make good decisions.

Learn to dismiss the demons and attract the awesome, and I am referring to your thoughts and what you may/may not be attracting into your life without even considering what you are actually doing.

Are you good at what you do? Whether it's in business, being a good friend, a loving and loyal partner. If you are good at what you do it's because you love what you are doing and you are always thinking about and subconsciously striving to make (attract) it better.

When people say 'money attracts money' it's the same process in operation when it comes to what you are thinking about; attracting love, friendship, a new career, luck, whatever it might be. The key to attracting what you desire is believing that you will receive it. Attraction and action go hand in hand. It's not enough to sit back on a Saturday night with your takeaway hoping that your life will improve. Take some form of action, a small step towards your goal.

If you don't try new techniques, new ways of thinking, your outcome will always be the same. Albert Einstein said that the definition of insanity is doing the same thing again and again and expecting different results. Attract what you want by firmly believing that it will happen.

The one thing we can't be specific about is time, exactly when something might happen. However, be specific about when you want something to happen but don't be too disheartened if it doesn't. Fate often interferes. This is possibly why most people give up. If you give up, you give in, and that's not the most attractive quality.

People are always attracted to those who

have a zest for life and know what they want. It's an attractive attribute.

The universe responds in the same way by guiding you and helping you. When someone next says to you that you are attractive, you can smile inwardly and know that the law of attraction is working for you.

True beauty truly is skin deep. Always accept a compliment if you believe it to be true.

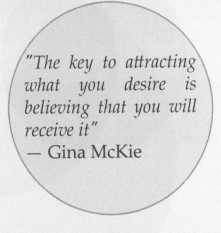

"The key to attracting what you desire is believing that you will receive it"
— Gina McKie

"Lots of people want to ride with you in the limo, but what you want is someone who will take the bus with you when the limo breaks down"
— Oprah Winfrey

THE
POWER
OF
SAYING
NO

IMAGINATION

How often have you said 'yes' to a person when your internal dialogue is screaming 'NO'?

You want to say 'no' but an inner-fear somehow takes over, warning you that a hostile reaction is coming your way, so suddenly you utter the word....'yes'; a false smile stretches across your face and you suddenly feel burdened, resentful, even victimised.

You might even quickly search for an excuse that you 'have just suddenly remembered' a reason why you need to say 'no' but alas, the agreement has been made and it's too late to retract the 'yes' word that has sealed an unwelcome commitment.

Why do we do it? Fear of rejection? The human desire to be liked? We think it will make us more popular? A willing person is a positive person? Whatever the reason, saying 'yes' on most occasions always plants a smile on someone else's face but perhaps not yours.

The instant gratification of saying 'yes' is a good feeling for both parties because you know that you are pleasing the other person, and a good deed has been done.

Then, that feeling of guilt starts to rise within you and you're subconsciously planning your escape route in a future conversation. Save yourself time and turmoil and learn to say 'no' effectively.

I was a yes person for many years: a

people pleaser. Suffice to say, not now. I would say yes to every task my boss would give me, 'yes' to the glamorous sales assistants offering me lotions and potions I really didn't need.

Then one day I said yes to going on a date with my brother's friend. I didn't want to go. I made myself ill with worry, I couldn't sleep, I felt sick and above all I just wished that I had said 'no'. I decided that I would practice saying 'no' and promised myself I would never put myself in this predicament again.

'Deliberate Practice' is a specifically defined term. It involves goal-setting, quick feedback, and countless drills to improve skills. 10,000 hours of deliberate practice will make you an expert at anything. In 95% of cases, natural talent does not determine who will become an expert at something. It's all about the practice. So I figured that I would become an expert at saying 'no'. It's not quite playing the drums or speaking a foreign language but it was a step in the right direction for me.

One day I decided to grace myself with the presence of the most persistent purposeful sales assistants at a large department store. I deliberately selected (from past experience) the most determined, persuasive women one could encounter in one afternoon. This was going to be my practice platform of saying 'no'. I left my purse at home; no money, just a large bag with nothing in it but my car keys and a large bottle of brain juice (water).

I was offered every amazing deal, discount, bargain that afternoon. The more I said 'no' the more I was offered. Of course I was tempted but I had no option, I had no money. Indeed, financially I was having a difficult time so I wasn't in a position to be making unnecessary purchases. At first, I bored myself (and the eager sales assistants) with excuses at the end of my 'no thank you' chat! I realised it was easier to simply say 'no', smile, and case closed.

Don't be the 'yes' person in your circle of friends, or at work. How often have you heard someone say, "Oh just get so and so to do it, they will say yes". Of course, say 'yes' if your aim is to deliver. If there is any doubt whatsoever, there is no harm in asking for time to think about your answer. This is a great way of buying extra time. Don't be put 'on the spot'.

Be true to yourself, say no when that is your answer. You are being honest and honesty is an admirable quality. Plus, you will feel liberated and have more time to do the things that really matter.

THE IMPORTANCE OF TAKING TIME OUT

IMAGINATION

From massage to meditation, there is a reason why we seek relaxation

Our minds and bodies need to rest. Not just sleeping, that is nature's way of ensuring we stay sane. We should never underestimate the power of sleep and the energy we get just from resting.

Forgoing sleep has huge health implications from obesity to heart disease, not to mention the importance of memory consolidation. This is why having a 'power nap' during the day can boost your health and mental well-being, yet most of us don't consider this to be an essential part of our daily living. There are many famous power nappers; Richard Branson, Margaret Thatcher, Bill Clinton and Winston Churchill to name but a few.

Research shows that napping can make you more alert, reduce stress and improve cognitive functioning by 40%. A nap should be between 15 and 30 minutes otherwise you fall into the deeper stages of sleep.

Recently my friend was telling me about the caffeine nap. I was excited to think that this involved a large latte with a blueberry muffin. No such luck. A caffeine nap (and she swears by this) is an intake of caffeine followed by a nap. Your body digests the caffeine while you are asleep and you wake up feeling refreshed. In order to do this, you must find a quiet place where both physically and mentally you can relax.

Milton H. Erickson was an American psychiatrist and psychologist. I respect his methods on all levels. His work focused on the effects of medical hypnosis and family therapy. He knew the powerful effects of napping and relaxing your mind through storytelling. Distraction is a wonderful tool which can boost your overall well-being. Have you ever been distracted by a song on the radio, reading an interesting article (like this one, hopefully), or someone telling you a great story? The latter was Ericsson's speciality.

I love the woodcutter story and often share this with clients. One sunny day, two woodcutters were in the woods and the younger chap said to the older chap that he was convinced he could cut more wood than him in a day. The older chap laughed, shook his head, and said he didn't believe him.

There was only one way to test the young

man's ambition. Set a challenge for both of them to cut wood. So, the following morning both men started to cut wood, eager to win the challenge. However, every 30 minutes or so, the elderly chap would sit down for a few minutes. The young chap observed this and smugly thought he just needed a rest. No resting for the young woodcutter, he didn't stop and ploughed his way through as much wood as the day would allow him to cut.

Finally, it was 'down tools time' for both woodcutters. There was a look of utter astonishment on the young chap's face as he noticed the older woodcutter had cut practically double the amount of wood compared to the young chap. The young woodcutter was confused and challenged the older woodcutter by telling him he watched him sitting down every 30 minutes or so. The older woodcutter smiled and said, "Yes I did sit down every 30 minutes or so, but I was taking time out to sharpen my saw."

Life is pretty much the same. Take time out for yourself. Plan this time. Oh, yes, and if you are ever caught snoozing on your desk at work because you have been out the night before, well just tell your boss that 'it's a power nap'!

For more information on author Gina McKie,
please visit www.ginamckie.com

A publication by Plan4 Media
www.plan4media.com